AlittleLIFEHAPPY
discovering the silver linings of life

—— Aakriti Ghai ——

First published by Busybird Publishing 2023

Copyright © 2023 Aakriti Ghai

ISBN: Paperback: 978-1-922954-17-6
Ebook: 978-1-922954-18-3

This book is copyright. Apart from any fair dealing for the purposes of study, research, criticism, review, or as otherwise permitted under the Copyright Act, no part may be reproduced by any process without written permission. Enquiries should be made through the publisher.

This is a work of fiction. Any similarities between places and characters are a coincidence.

Cover image: Lillian Busby

Cover design: Busybird Publishing

Layout and typesetting: Busybird Publishing

Editor: Krystle Herdy

Busybird Publishing
2/118 Para Road
Montmorency, Victoria
Australia 3094
www.busybird.com.au

*Dedicated to everyone in
search of meaning.*

Let's walk together.

AlittleLIFEHAPPY

I believe that words heal.
I have seen that words give comfort.

I hope these poems act as a companion that supports you and helps you find meaning in any hurdles you may face on your journey.

I hope you will find joy and poetry in the simplicity of life.
Take in these words and feel the joy.

Keep this book in your pocket and read it whenever life calls you to it.

Aakriti Ghai

Contents

Finding Meaning	1
If Love Had an Address	2
Eternal Optimist	3
Constellations	4
I am Love, I am Light	5
Hope Shines	6
Shine Your Light	7
A Cage	8
Summer	9
Small Things	10
Shadow	11
Blooming Positivity	12
Prisoner of the Mind	13
This Path	14
My Tears and Me	15
Envy Isn't Pretty	16
The Monsters under My Bed	17
A Book with No Cover	18
This Bench and Me	19
Phases of the Moon	20
The Gift	21
The Power Within You	22
A Landscape	23
Flow Freely	24
Beautiful Views	25

When Everything is Alright	26
Leaves Leave Too	27
Silver Linings	28
My Words	29
Shades of Yesterday	30
Heart and the World of Art	31
No Free Rides	32
Liberation	33
Hope Breathes	34
Manuscript of My Life	35
I Feel Every Feel	36
With The Colours Of	37
Serenity	38
Girls Together	39
Paradise	40
Trying	41
Compassion	42
Satire of my Fear	43
Temporary Heaven	44
Road That I Am On	45
New Beginnings	46
Is It Me?	47
Life's Joys	48
Your First Love	49
Ocean Hits Rocks	50
Time and Space	51
I Don't Want to go Back	52

Finding Meaning

I have never agreed with meaninglessness
Always a nomad running

wild in the search for meaning
My questions remain unanswered
I never seem to find
meaning to these questions of life

I am often told to just let it be
but I don't agree
Nomadic it may seem
searching for meaning on a journey
that may never be complete

If Love Had an Address

If love had an address
it would be somewhere that
feels like home
Safe and secure
you would feel whole

Love is how love feels

If love had an address
it would be in the comfort
that love provides

Love is how love feels

Love is different for you and me
for Mum and me
for Dad and me
My grandmother made me feel it
all around me

Love has countless residents because
Love is how love feels
If love had an address
It would have a different residence for me

Eternal Optimist

A happy wish
Eternal optimist
Lights that won't be missed

I don't understand those
who try to diminish
a happy wish fulfilled

A painting of my mind
I will see in sight
a canvas of the
eternal optimist

I don't understand those
who try to diminish
a happy wish

Eternal optimist
Oh, how I wish
for you to make a happy wish

Constellations

I see the vast dark night
nothing left, nothing in sight

Flashing
high in the sky
I see my life

Contemplating
everything that has gone
I see constellations
shining far away
They blow my mind

Stars shimmering in the distance
make me wonder
why I ever thought
I wouldn't find a way

The moonless night will
always have its shine

Constellations will rise
from every vast dark night

I am Love, I am Light

I am love, I am light
I won't let anyone
tell me otherwise

I do fall, I do fight
Every light loses its shine
if it doesn't love its life

I am love, I am light
I live and seek to return
love and light

I do fall, I do fight
Life loses its shine
if lived selfishly

I am love, I am light
I hope to always give
I hope to always receive
this love and light

Hope Shines

What I seek
I dream
I paint with a hope that
shines within me

A luminous illusion
glows inside me
A hope that shines
with a supernova's might

I hope to always have hope
illuminating inside me
A hope that shines
with a supernova's might

Shine Your Light

Shine your light
bright
It shall
ignite and unite
taking you to new heights

Dreaming and beaming
shine your light
ignite a mind
that unites you
with the beams
of your dreams
every night

A Cage

I want to be free to be me
Don't stop what I ought to be
I won't be caged in greed

Let me be free
Your cage destroys
what I set out to be
It confines me
It takes away parts of me
I wish to keep

A cage is simply a way to feed
the greed of people who themselves
have never been free

Summer

I always long for summer
one that shields me like armour
Yellow tones seeking
bright hues
Summer is always
too good to be true

I wish for it
always knowing
summer is around
somewhere
and it will come back to me
after every winter ends

Small Things

I love the small things:
reading enchanting lines
musing to music at night
sipping my tea
laughing with a friend

When I go on with my small things
a simple thought crosses my mind
These small things make life so full
so why do I treat them as small things?

I hope I always love my small things
They will keep me full
even if it all
comes to a shallow end

Shadow

Walking in a city so
alien from my past
my shadow following
I saw a path
that tugged at my heart

This shadow of mine
holds me back
not wanting me to leave
to march ahead on the path

My shadow and I
have always harboured conflicts
We are the only constant
on these alien paths

I move forward
my shadow on every path
constant and conflictual

Blooming Positivity

I am averse to gloomy sights
my soul within carries a happy vibe

gloom comes
It tries to switch the happy 'I'
not knowing

I am eternal sunshine
that will always carry
this ecstatic high

Prisoner of the Mind

My mind is a vast land
that recalls everything once said
It sprints in a race against itself
only stopping to wander through
notions
I'd thought I'd conquered

My mind creates and feels at ease
but ends up eating itself away
with thoughts from times long gone

I live inside my head
straining to scrub away
difficult things heard and said

My mind is a vast land
that just wants to dream and create
to break free
from fear and past chains

This Path

I like this path
the one I came from
the one I am travelling on
I don't know what there was
or what there will be, but

I like the path in between

I am a crusader
marching forward
down this path
on a journey that
fulfils me to no end

My Tears and Me

We meet often
my tears and me
My emotions come out

Like wind in a storm
we feel every feel

These tears form me
they make me human
my tears make me real

Envy Isn't Pretty

Envy isn't pretty
It comes out
in ropes used to
pull others down

Love your life so fully
Have the sense to
absorb only what
comes to you happily

Envy isn't pretty
It reeks of hatred
Disturbingly petty
envy is never pretty

The Monsters Under My Bed

The monsters under my bed
scream from far and near
shouting the words
I am afraid to hear

The monsters under my bed
squeal and make me shrug
bringing back things
I'd shoved under the rug

The monsters under my bed
know what I am afraid to say
They keep me up and wide-awake
I wish they would stay away

The monsters under my bed
cause me to jump and hide
for it is only at night the monsters
all come alive in my mind

A Book with No Cover

I am a book with no cover
Words swim out and hover

A book should not be judged
because it is not hidden by
beauty that meets the eye

This book with no cover
has words and depth to wonder
This book with no cover
here for your eyes to wander

This Bench and Me

This bench and me
we wonder, we ponder
sharing stories
just us and the peace
lingering on

This bench and me
seem to find each other easily
our tied chemistry
bringing me calming solitude

This bench and me
come together naturally
creating stories
oh so beautifully

Phases of the Moon

The moon grows from nothingness
then emerges through phases
half-hidden, half in sight

Centre of the blank night
I wonder why it shines so bright
only to disappear again

Phases of the moon
like phases of a life
shine bright
only to disappear one night

I understand now
the moon merges with my life
Still, I don't forgive the phases
that came and went

Phases of the moon
that lead to it glowing bright
embrace every darkness
until it reaches its full moonlight

The Gift

the gift of solitude
the taste of being so you
a gift you discover within

the gift of solitude
the residents residing in you
a gift you can only discover within

The Power Within You

Power lies within you
Aspirations and hopes
You must make them come true

Your power tells you that
only you can make your
hopes and dreams come true

Power lies within you
so just believe in
what your power tells you

A Landscape

I am painting
my mindscape
or is it
my escape?

It is a habit
My mind is
a canvas
calling the hands of an artist

I am painting
a landscape
from the colours of
my wishes

I become the artist
coating my canvas with
the colours of desire

I am painting
always
my escape
my own landscape

Flow Freely

I have cultivated
my journey
every step of the way

A life of strength
hard work and simple progress
Independence leads to freedom
Life is meant to be experienced

Flowing free
happy and content
I hope to always move forward
with a spirit that flows freely

Beautiful Views

Beautiful views
blue hues
a bird flying too

I want to
understand
to seek the sky

My dreams
are an eagle flying
across a secluded golden beach

Through changing views
I am proud
to have found my way

Aakriti Ghai

When Everything is Alright

A void
Avoid
A feeling
Fleeting
Walls high

It's alright
when everything is all right
to feel
a void
you want to avoid

Flee the feeling
Time flies
Life proposes
walls so high
even when
everything is alright

Leaves Leave Too

Leaves leave
in peace
They fall
to the ground
merging all around

Leaves grow again
from their branches
they blossom
through sun or rain

New leaves in the trees
muse and move
with the wind and rain
but they leave too

Leaves in peace
fall to the ground
just to grow back
once again

Aakriti Ghai

Silver Linings

Torn or discoloured
my drawings
always have
potential

In my sketches
I somehow
always find
the silver lining

My Words

We keep company
Addicted to the solitude
I feel so full
No company has
made me feel so free

I am complete
This one doesn't judge me
I put it to paper
the sweet love story
of my words and me

Shades of Yesterday

Shades of yesterday
still meet me today

I see
hues of what was
in the colours
of what I do today

Shades of yesterday
reflect on the outline
of my palette today

Heart and the World of Art

Inhale an idea
Exhale a creation
Breathe in and breathe out
a concept of your heart

I see art
in the simplest of days
in the cities I visit
in the lives that our
greatest creator created

Inhale an idea
Exhale a creation
It is a privilege
to see and feel art
to inhale and exhale
to feel with a heart
in a world of creation

No Free Rides

Pull up your socks
even when they keep
coming down
Don't whine
You must
plough through

Pull up your socks
even when they keep
falling down
There are
no free rides
allowed

Liberation

I fall down
infinitely
but always
pick myself up
and try
to get better

I keep dreaming
I keep believing
I know I will fall
but when I
pick myself up
it is liberation
that remains

Aakriti Ghai

Hope Breathes

I exhale dreams
breathe in whims and fancies
Hope inhales
It tells me
Breathe
Let life in
Exhale your dreams
patiently

Manuscript of My Life

Destiny prescribed
Experiences recited
The manuscript of my life
somehow designed
in hindsight

Manuscript of my life
even now I would not
edit out anything
that life has transcribed

I Feel Every Feel

It's okay to feel every feeling
Tear with every tear
It's okay to
feel the pangs of every fear

Face that fear
here and now
feel what was and
what is coming still

I feel every feeling
too deep
Every up and down
keeps me full and wondering

how we become so empty
so shallow that
we can no longer
call ourselves human

With The Colours Of

Paint me with the colours of
trust and honesty
love and individuality
gratitude and fullness

Paint me with the colours of
something more than meets the eye
I have searched and rarely found
these colours around

I seek them all the time
but hardly ever find
the colours I hope to see
the colours that paint me

Paint me with the colours of
a fullness so rare to find
Shallowness is something
that will never be with me or mine

Serenity

Strive for sweet memories
Pray for clarity
Compose your scenery
Hear calm melodies
Absorb sharp storms gracefully
Strive for small epiphanies
Live it

Strive for serenity

Girls Together

My girls build me up
for a girl and a girl
grow and glow
in this world
together

My girls and I
often chatter about and conquer
the curves life throws at us
together

I have their backs and
they have mine
We stand tall
together

Sisterhood is wonderful
I walk with my girls
in every weather
often wondering
what we would do
if we did not have each other

Paradise

They say
we shall reunite
in paradise
just me and mine

Humans tell stories
faith helps them survive

I want to believe in
the stories told
because I want to
reunite with my departed
in paradise

Trying

I am trying
I am becoming
a new version of myself

I work hard
to see
a version of me
that would make
earlier versions
proud

I am trying
for a new version of myself
I am working every day

Compassion

compassion is the heart of all
compassion should be in and for all beings

compassion should be omnipresent
compassion is a virtue

compassion was possessed by legends
compassion is for the suffering and hating

compassion can heal
compassion is a human state of being

Satire of my Fear

A satire of my fear
a tiring mimic of
the creature
I hate to hear

My mind
yearns to conquer
the image of my fear

I do not wish to
see or hear
this simple being

but it rests within me
This creature
a satire of my fear
I do not want to bear

Temporary Heaven

Creation and appreciation
Musings and amusement
A temporary heaven
where I find solace
where I am me:

perfectly imperfect

Messy and abundant
Loving and caring
I create and seek at
every moment
in my temporary heaven

Road That I Am On

The road that I am walking
seems to go on

Passersby travel along
but eventually continue without me

I just go on
with the ones who
want to come along
down this road that I am on

New Beginnings

A clean page
A clean slate
Fresh ground for
new spaces

I am curious
when it comes
to new beginnings

We can compose
new pages
at any age

Until our last breaths
we are given the chance
to write upon
fresh clean pages

Is It Me?

Set me free
Be with me

Don't make me hollow
I want to be free

For that you will have to
connect with me

My heart
was not made
for this shallow story

Life's Joys

I wonder:
if life comes to us only once
and just for a short while
why do we look
for different highs
instead of just accepting
the little joys that come by?

Your First Love

Fall in love with yourself
Your journey is precious
one that belongs only to you

You may hear demeaning words
from loudmouths
waiting for your fall

Don't let them make you forget
the magic of your soul and
the experiences that have shaped you

Your first love
is your reflection in the mirror
There is strength
in the beautiful eyes
staring back at you

Ocean Hits Rocks

Ocean hits rocks
flows towards them
on its own
flowing back and forth

Ocean hits rocks
All through its course
ocean flows and goes
it never halts

Back and forth it flows
Ocean never halts
no matter
how many rocks

Time and Space

What goes around
comes back
always in a loop
What you go through at one time
leads you to another

Through thick and thin
what happens in one moment
manifests again in another

Time and space are
concepts that play
beautifully
whether good or bad
in front of our eyes

I Don't Want to go Back

So far, so good

Should I go back to tell myself
I made it this far?

Why would I want to go back?

Keep moving along
away from what is far gone

Take me back only to remember
For recollection and reflection

but I won't stay there
I will go on to say

I don't want to go back
not after coming so far

www.ingramcontent.com/pod-product-compliance
Lightning Source LLC
Chambersburg PA
CBHW041310110526
44590CB00028B/4313